CATHOLIC
PRAYER BOOK
for
Mothers

Donna-Marie Cooper O'Boyle

Our Sunday Visitor Publishing Division
Our Sunday Visitor, Inc.
Huntington, IN 46750

Nihil Obstat:
Rev Michael Heintz, *Censor Librorum*

Imprimatur:
✠John M. D'Arcy
Bishop of Fort Wayne-South Bend
July 27, 2005

Copyright © 2005 by Our Sunday Visitor Publishing Division,
Our Sunday Visitor, Inc. Published 2005.
14 13 12   5 6 7 8 9

Our Sunday Visitor Publishing Division
Our Sunday Visitor, Inc.
200 Noll Plaza
Huntington, IN 46750

ISBN: 1-59276-161-5 (Inventory No. T212)
LCCN: 2005926031
Cover design by Monica Haneline
Interior design by Sherri L. Hoffman

PRINTED IN THE UNITED STATES OF AMERICA

Dedicated with great love . . .

To my five children, Justin, Chaldea, Jessica, Joseph, and Mary-Catherine. They are all wonderful, unique, and beautiful human beings. They have given me great joy and loving direction in my vocation as a mother. I thoroughly enjoy my journey with them.

To my mother, Alexandra Mary Uzwiak Cooper, and my father, Eugene Joseph Cooper, in loving memory and in thanksgiving for bringing me into this world.

In loving memory of my deceased brother, Gary John Cooper.

To my dear friend, Reverend William Smith, who is a great source of inspiration and guidance.

To my husband, David, for his love and support. He is the wind beneath my wings.

And lastly, I dedicate this prayer book in honor and loving memory of two "saints" of our time: Blessed Teresa of Calcutta, whom I had the great privilege of knowing, and our late Holy Father, Pope John Paul II, who holds a very special place in my heart.

Encouraging words about this book
to the author from
Blessed Teresa of Calcutta:

"My gratitude is my prayer for you that you may grow in the love of God through your beautiful thoughts of prayer you write and thus share with others."

"Your books on mothers and expectant mothers are much needed. Yes, you may use some of the things I said on motherhood and family. . . . I pray that God may bless your endeavors."

"God has given you many gifts — make sure you use them for the glory of God and the good of the people. You will then make your life something beautiful for God. You have been created to be Holy. I assure you of my prayers and hope you pray for me also. Keep the joy of loving Jesus ever burning in your heart and share this joy with others."

About this book, Blessed Teresa of Calcutta also said, "I pray that it does much good."

Table Of Contents

Introduction

How could anyone begin to explain the countless inde- scribable blessings, joys, and rewards interwoven in the tapestry of motherhood? Along with these remarkable moments in a mother's life, of course, are also woven the sacrifices and sorrows; even in these, God's grace abounds to mothers just for the asking. Our Lord certainly favors mothers. After all, He actually enters into a partnership with them to create human life. What an incredible mys- tery and miracle!

Adoptive mothers, stepmothers, and godmothers, as partners in this mystery, can also benefit from beseeching our Lord for His assistance. Their prayers help ensure that their influence on the children in their lives will be holy, and they will find joy and peace in their particular and important roles.

Whatever mothering role she plays, the power of a mother's prayer cannot be underestimated. And our good Lord also knows you would welcome more time for prayer and quiet times to listen to His promptings in your soul. But a busy household can be very far from quiet, and time itself can seem to be a luxury. It would actually be wrong for a mother to drop everything to kneel down to pray. Especially as her baby is crying for her attention, a sick child is in need of her care, or her family is waiting for din- ner. A mother's time is truly not her own.

So how does a mother remain faithful to prayer and yet keep up with her work around the clock in the home? The key to inner peace for a mother is to find a balance between a prayer life and her duties and care of her family. A faithful mother soon learns that in order to survive, her life should become a prayer.

Prayer has three forms of expression: vocal, meditative, and contemplative. All forms come from the heart. All bring us closer to God.

Vocal prayer is a common form of prayer, used often and founded on the union of body and soul. It can be used alone or in a group.

Meditative prayer is actually a pursuit, seeking to understand Christian life and principles in order to follow and adhere to them. Our thoughts, emotions, and imagination are engaged as we learn about our faith from Sacred Scripture, the lives of the saints, and spiritual reading.

Contemplation is, according to St. Teresa of Ávila, "Nothing else than a close sharing between friends; it means taking time frequently to be alone with him who we know loves us." The *Catechism of the Catholic Church* says, "Contemplation is a gaze of faith, fixed on Jesus." A mother finds the need to lift her mind and heart to our Lord often throughout her day for strength, grace and guidance. He is always waiting for her heart ready to listen to her pleas.

The Lord will speak to the silence of a mother's heart when she retreats to that place in her heart to love, worship, listen to, and gaze upon Him who gives us life. Mothers are truly contemplatives in the heart of the family and in the world.

Allow this prayer book to assist you in keeping your heart always lifted up toward Heaven, communicating with the Divine, even as your hands are occupied with household and motherly tasks. May God bless you and your beautiful family!

CHAPTER ONE

Precious Blessings

"For this child I prayed; and the Lord has granted me my petition which I made to him. Therefore I have lent him to the Lord; as long as he lives, he is lent to the Lord."
— 1 SAM. 1:27, 28

The Beautiful Gift of Motherhood

Dear Lord Jesus, thank you for the beautiful gift of motherhood, one of the greatest gifts ever. At times, I feel unworthy of this awesome task of raising Christian children. Other times, I may be so busy with their care, I even forget the great privilege that motherhood really is. Please enlighten my mind and senses and help me to renew my resolve in being the mother I am destined to be.

The moral and spiritual strength of a woman is joined to her awareness that God entrusts to her, in a special way, the human being.

— POPE JOHN PAUL II

A Glimpse Into the Future

If a woman could ever get a glimpse at
What her world would be
When she becomes a mother,
She would be presented with the reality
That her innermost desires and life plans
would be altered or put on hold
because she would be inundated with the care of others.
If she was also allowed to glimpse the unending joy
she would receive as a mother,

There would be no pause to consider,
No hesitation, as she embraced the whole package,
Knowing in her heart that her children will *become* her
 life's desires.

The child is the beauty of God present in the world, the
greatest gift to the family.
 — BLESSED TERESA OF CALCUTTA

Bless me, Lord. Be with me, Lord.
 I need You, Lord.

Mother's Daily Prayer for Her Children

O Mary, Immaculate Virgin, Mother of our Lord Jesus
Christ, Patroness of all mothers, I commend my beloved
children to the Most Sacred Heart of your Son, Jesus and
to your Immaculate Heart. Please assist our family and
keep us always in your care. Please protect us from the
snares of the devil and keep us on the road that leads to
Life. Help me to realize my sublime mission as mother and
help me to be faithful to my duties for the good of my family and the good of the entire family of God.

 Most Sacred Heart of Jesus, have mercy on us.
 Immaculate Heart of Mary, pray for us.
 Holy Guardian Angel of our family, pray for us.
 St. Michael, pray for us.

St. Joseph, husband of Mary, pray for us.
St. Anne, Mother of Mary, pray for us.
St. Monica, pray for us.
St. Gerard Majella, pray for us.
Blessed Teresa of Calcutta, pray for us.

With Every Step I Praise You

As I am carrying my baby and rocking her to sleep,
You know, Lord, that I am unable
To kneel down at this moment to pray.
Please listen to the prayer of love in my heart for You.
Let each of my steps throughout this day
Be in honor and praise of You.
Allow my hands, please to serve You
As I tend to my family's needs.
Help me to continue to see You in my family
And recognize the sublime mission I have as a mother.

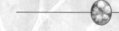

Prayer to the Blessed Mother

Dear Blessed Mother Mary, Mother of Jesus and my mother, help me to learn to become more prayerful as I mother my children. Please inspire me to imitate your virtues and to lift my heart toward Heaven often, asking your Son, Jesus, for the graces I need to be the mother I should be. Please remind me to pray, especially when I feel overwhelmed and overtired. Help me to be a shining example to my children.

A Reflection on the Miraculous Vocation of Motherhood

From the moment you found out that you were carrying a child in your womb, your motherly heart enlarged in response to this new life. Take some time to reflect on the amazing and miraculous vocation of motherhood, God has given you with this truly incredible gift . . . the care of another human being! One who looks to you for love, guidance and direction . . . one who depends on you for his very life!

CHAPTER TWO

A Mother's Love—
The Greatest Gift

*Love is patient and kind; love is not jealous or boast-
ful; it is not arrogant or rude. Love does not insist on
its own way; it is not irritable or resentful; it does not
rejoice at wrong, but rejoices in the right. Love bears
all things, believes all things, hopes all things, endures
all things. Love never ends ... So, faith, hope, love
abide, these three; but the greatest of these is love.*
— 1 COR. 13:4-8,13

Love is by its nature the primary gift, from which all other gifts follow.

— St. Thomas Aquinas

Nourished By Your Life and Love

Your child knew your love even before she saw the light of day. She was rocked by your every move as she resided in your womb, waiting to be born into this world, to be able to look into your comforting eyes. She was nourished by your life and love and continues to be now. What an incredible miracle of God!

Motherhood involves a special communion with the mystery of life, as it develops in the mother's womb. The mother is filled with wonder at this mystery of life, and understands with unique intuition what is happening inside her. In the light of the beginning the mother accepts and loves as a person the child she is carrying in her womb.

— Pope John Paul II

Mother's Loving Hands

God made mother's hands
To Love,
To cuddle, to hold, to caress,
To Love,
To bathe, to feed, to keep warm,
To Love,
To clothe, to mend,
To Love,
To clean, to cook, to fix,
To Love,
To build, to play, to share,
To Love,
To nurture, to hold tight, to teach,
To Love,
To discipline, to embrace, to pick up,
To Love,
To stroke, to tickle,
To Love,
To draw close, to comfort, to encourage,
To Love,
To wipe away tears, to help, to bless,
To Love,
To raise up little saints to heaven,
     To love ... to love ... to love.

Love cannot remain by itself — it has no meaning. Love has to be put into action and that action is service. How do we put the love for God in Action? By being faithful to our family, to the duties that God has entrusted to us.
— Blessed Teresa of Calcutta

A Spiritual Communion

My Jesus, I believe that You are present in the most Holy Sacrament. I love You above all things and I desire to receive You into my soul. Since I cannot at this moment receive You sacramentally, come at least spiritually into my heart. I embrace You as if You are already there and unite myself wholly to You; never permit me to be separated from You.

Dear Blessed Mother Mary,
teach me to love my children
with a heavenly love.

Lord Jesus, please help me to look for some inner stillness and silence in my heart to seek Your grace as I go about my busy schedule. Help me to realize the special communion I have with the mystery of life that has been bestowed upon me. Help me to see that even the smallest act, done with great love, is perfect in Your eyes.

A Reflection on a Mother's Love

Take some time to reflect on a mother's love and how your heart has grown because of the children in your life. Ask Our dear Lord, in your own words, for wisdom, insight, and all the graces needed to be the mother He wants you to be.

CHAPTER THREE

Holy Nurturing

. . . love one another earnestly from the heart.
— 1 PET. 1:22

Dear Lord Jesus, help me to see how much I influence other lives through my own life. These human beings, the gift of children You have given me, are totally dependent on me from even before they came into this world, and because of a mother's love, even continue to be dependent in some ways as adults. Please grant me the graces I most need as the mother of my children. Help me to be the prayerful and loving example I should be. I pray for insight, wisdom, strength and patience to love and nurture my little ones with holiness. Thank You for the incredible gift of life!

Let us always whisper His name of love as an antidote to all the discord that surrounds us. The harmony of heaven begins for us while, silent from the world, we again and again repeat, "Jesus, Jesus, Jesus!"

— St. Elizabeth Seton

Jesus, Jesus, Jesus,
I love you.

Patience

It takes a little patience...
To wait for your little one
Who has been stirring within your womb
For nine months waiting to be born.

It takes a little patience...
To wait for your baby,
Who has his days and nights reversed,
To get on the proper cycle.

It takes a little patience...
To wait for your baby
To sleep a little more through the night.

It takes a little patience...
With yourself
To get back into shape
After having given birth.

It takes a little patience...
On Dad's part
With Mom
As she regains her strength,
So she will be back to her "old" self again.

It takes a little patience...
Walking the floors with a colicky baby.

It takes a little patience...
With a little one
Who demands your full attention.

It takes a little patience...
With yourself as you strive to
Reschedule your day
According to your little one's schedule.

It takes a little patience...
Dealing with toddlers
Who have "minds of their own."

It takes a little patience...
Coping with and correcting
The bickering in the home
And sibling rivalry.

It takes a little patience...
Guiding teenaged children
Who are trying to find their way
Without your help.

It takes a little patience...
Keeping peace in the home.

Dear Lord, grant me, please, the virtue of patience!

Blessed Mother Mary, thank you
for guiding me in holiness.

A Reflection
on Holy Nurturing

*Take some time to reflect on your
role as a mother. Consider how your
faith influences the way you mother your
child. Consider also the importance prayer,
so necessary for survival, has in your life
and the life of your family. Consider how a
Christian mother sees the need to not only
nurture her child with love, but with
holiness as well. Ask Our Lord, in your
own words, for all of the grace
necessary to be the mother
you should be.*

CHAPTER FOUR

First Teacher

"You are the light of the world. A city set on a hill cannot be hid. Nor do men light a lamp and put it under a bushel, but on a stand, and it gives light to all in the house. Let your light so shine before men, that they may see your good works and give glory to your Father who is in heaven."
— MT. 5:14-16

Dear Jesus, thank You for the precious gifts of my children. Help me to remember to call upon You and Your Blessed Mother often for guidance and direction in my role as first teacher. Although my days are filled to capacity most times with all the important "stuff" I feel I need to do as mother, help me to realize the need to look upward for help and grace. Thank you for the natural motherly sentiments You have put in my soul. Help me to build upon them with Your grace.

Dear Mother Mary,
teach me to teach my children
in righteousness.

Blessed Guardians, be watchful. Help us to use well the graces of the moment in the care and instruction of little ones under our charge. Watch over them with us.
— St. Elizabeth Seton

We must "introduce" our children to their guardian angels and stress the importance of a relationship with them.

Angel of God
Angel of God, my Guardian Dear,
To Whom God's love commits me here.

Ever this day (night) be at my side,
To light and guard,
To rule and guide.
Amen.

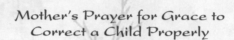

Mother's Prayer for Grace to Correct a Child Properly

Dear Lord, along with the incredible gift of motherhood comes the sacred and weighty responsibility in teaching and correcting my children. Help me to never shirk from my duty of correction according to Your holy will. May I realize that I take Your place and speak for You, so may I be worthy of that trust. Help me never correct my children in anger, but always in a calm and motherly manner, and punish with a gentle firmness born of tender mother love. Amen.

The Most Essential Teachings

Dear Lord, help me to see that some of the most essential teachings to my impressionable children are in my example and actions. My actions are much more articulate than my words can ever be. Some of the most important lessons in life are learned when watching one who is respected and loved. Help me to be mindful of my choices and the critical examples I give my children. Remind me, too that my prayer life spills over into my family and will help to enhance their grasp of prayer and their understanding of what is most essential.

A Reflection on Being the First Teacher

Take some time to reflect on your role as your child's first teacher. Consider all you are teaching your children, by word and example. Consider what you should be teaching them. Ask Our Lord, in your own words, for help and guidance. He will give it to you for the asking. He will grant you every grace you need.

CHAPTER FIVE

The Heart of the Home

*"A new commandment I give to you, that you love one
another; even as I have loved you, that you also love
one another. By this all men will know that you are
my disciples, if you have love for one another."*
— JN. 13: 34-36

A mother exists at the heart of the home, the center of the hub, reaching out to all around her. She is the source of comfort and solace, love and guidance. A mother is involved in many roles, the most significant being the heart in the center of home life. She anchors the ship in the stormy sea of life. She radiates joy to her children. She balances the scales of family life. Although, unfortunately in our world a mother's role is very much devalued, our Lord knows the intrinsic value of motherhood. We should also.

Dear Lord Jesus, help me to stay focused and patient in my mothering. It is a mothering that comes naturally, but also calls for grace and guidance from You. Help me to be open to your graces for me as a mother. Please give me confidence in knowing that I am doing exactly what You have destined me to do in the mothering of my children. Help me to bring back, by my love and example in my home and the world, the true value that motherhood deserves. Let my example inspire other mothers who may be struggling for direction. Amen.

In My Laundry Room

As I carefully fold my sheets,
Smoothing out the wrinkles,
Bringing corner to corner . . .
Lovingly, I think of You, my Lord.

The pile of laundry seemingly grows beside me,
As I strive to keep up
With this never-ending chore.

But, in my laundry room ...
I thank You, my dear Lord,
For loving me and allowing me
To serve You in my family.

O Mary, my Mother, be with me throughout
my vocation and teach me to be open
to God's grace for me, even when I am
seemingly running through these
days of motherhood.

Prayer of St. Francis of Assisi

Lord, make me an instrument of Your peace.
Where there is hatred, let me sow love;
Where there is injury, pardon;
Where there is doubt, faith;
Where there is despair, hope;
Where there is darkness, light;
And where there is sadness, joy.

O Divine Master, grant that I may not so much seek to be
consoled as to console; to be understood as to understand;
to be loved as to love. For it is in giving that we receive, it

is in pardoning that we are pardoned, and it is in dying that we are born to eternal life.

Dear Lord Jesus, thank you for the blessings of my family. My motherhood gives me so many opportunities to joyfully grow along with my children. Please give me strength when I am weary. Help me to radiate joy to my family so they may be uplifted and be able to spread that joy to others.

A Reflection on the Heart of the Home

Remember that prayers can be said as a mother goes about her day in the care of the family. Prayers do not need to be formal or elaborate, but should come from the heart. Get into the habit of raising your thoughts from time to time throughout the day, conversing with Jesus and His Blessed Mother. They are always readily available to hear your thoughts and pleas.

CHAPTER SIX

The Holy Family

Finally, all of you, have unity of spirit,
sympathy, love of the brethren, a tender heart
and a humble mind.
— 1 PET. 3:8-9

D ear Lord Jesus, help me to consider the life of the Holy Family. Please give my family the grace to imitate their virtues. I know that our family is certainly not the Holy Family, but I pray that we can become holy in the way You want us to be. Help us to find the simplicity in our living and approach the life of our family with a clear purpose I mind. Help us to see that we are a unique unit of people brought together by You, where we work out our salvation together. I pray for Your holy will in our lives. Amen.

The Church of the Home

God gives us the example of the Holy Family
Who lived, worked and prayed together
Humbly, quietly and lovingly
Caring for each other in Nazareth.

We can strive to imitate their holiness,
And pray for their heavenly intercession,
Prayers should be taught to our children from birth,
They will become as natural as breathing.

The home should be a place of peace and tranquility
Where the family can retreat away from the world.
We encounter God there,
His presence is felt there,
His love is known there.

The family — above all — is the special place of the human person, it provides the environment in which the person is conceived, is born, and grows . . . the context of the person's earthly happiness and human hope.

— POPE JOHN PAUL II

A Reflection on a Mother's Role in Her Family

Take some time to reflect on the awesome role you have as mother of your family, as the nucleus of that group of people that God has brought together. Try to develop a plan for prayer. Prayer, a conversation with the Divine, is always appropriate at any time. Raising your heart and mind to God can be done whenever you want...while going about your work or at quiet times. Think about the Holy Family and their prayerful attitude about life. Let us pray, as mothers to be the guide for our families to help them reach their final destiny.

CHAPTER SEVEN

An Imitation of the Blessed Mother

But Mary kept all these things, pondering them in her heart.
— Lk. 2:19

The Blessed Mother ... Jesus's Mother, our Holy Mother, and Mother of the Church. She is a true source of unending strength and peace for us all. A Mother who never grows weary of our pleas. A Mother whose protection is immense, limitless..whose guidance awaits us. Never hesitate to call upon the Blessed Mother.

Dear Lord Jesus, You who lived with your Blessed Mother Mary in Bethlehem and Nazareth... You, who are God, experienced her motherly love in ways You want even me to experience. Please remind me that I can call upon Your Mother for help, guidance, and protection. Amen.

The *Memorare*

Remember, O most gracious Virgin Mary, that never was it known that anyone who fled to your protection, implored your help, or sought your intercession was left unaided. Inspired by this confidence I fly unto you, O virgin of virgins, my Mother. To you do I come, before you I stand, sinful and sorrowful. O Mother of the Word Incarnate, despise not my petitions, but in your mercy, hear and answer me. Amen.

— PRAYER BY ST. BERNARD OF CLAIRVAUX

Like Mary, we must allow the Holy Spirit to help us become intimate friends of Christ.

— POPE JOHN PAUL II

Mary, Mother of God

Hail Mary, Mother of Christ and of the Church!
Hail our life, our sweetness, and our hope!

To your care, I entrust the necessities of all families,
The joys of children, the desires of the young,
The worries of adults, the pain of the sick,
The serene old age of senior citizens!

I entrust to you the fidelity of your Son's ministers,
The hope of all those preparing themselves for this
    ministry,
The joyous dedication of virgins in cloisters,
The prayer and concern of men and women religious,
The lives and commitment of all those who work for
    Christ's reign on earth.

— POPE JOHN PAUL II

Roses For You

Dear Blessed Mother, please accept each of my motherly
    tasks this day
as a little act of love. Let them be as roses to be put at
    your feet, one by one.
I pray that by the end of the day, there will be an
    enormous bouquet to adorn your feet.

A Reflection on the Imitation of the Blessed Mother

Take some time each day to pray to the Blessed Mother. Ask her often to assist you in allowing the Holy Spirit to help you become an intimate friend of Jesus. Ask her to give you reminders to pray as you go about your busy days in the care of your family. The Blessed Mother wants to mother you. In the words of Blessed Teresa of Calcutta, "Mary, Mother of Jesus, be a mother to me now."

CHAPTER EIGHT

Wisdom of the Saints

*Therefore, my beloved brothers, be steadfast,
immovable, always abounding in the work
of the Lord, knowing that in the Lord
your labor is not in vain.*
— 1 COR. 15:58

The family of saints, in Heaven and on earth, gives us an example of holiness to imitate. There are those who have gone before us, declared to be saints by the Church, and those holy ones living in our midst. We can become a prayerful people, lifting our hearts and minds to God, striving to imitate the virtues of the saints.

Consecrating Our Children to St. Joseph

O glorious St. Joseph, to you God committed the care of
   His only-begotten Son, amid the many dangers of
   this world.
We come to you and ask you to take under your special
   protection the children God has given us.
Through holy Baptism, they became children of God
   and members of His holy Church.
We consecrate them to you today, that through this
   consecration they may become your foster children.
Guard them, guide their little steps in life, and form
   their hearts after the hearts of Jesus and Mary.
St. Joseph, you who felt the tribulation and worry of a
   parent when the Child Jesus was lost, protect our
   dear children for time and eternity.
May you be their father and counselor.
Let them, like Jesus grow in age as well as wisdom and
   grace before God and men.

Preserve them from the corruption of this world, and
    give us the grace one day to be united with them in
    heaven forever.
Amen.

Prayer to St. Michael

St. Michael the Archangel, defend us in battle; be our protection against the wickedness and snares of the devil. May
God rebuke him, we humbly pray, and do thou, O Prince
of the Heavenly Host, by the divine power of God, cast
into hell Satan and all the evil spirits who roam through
the world seeking the ruin of souls. Amen.

Invocation to St. Thérèse

O Glorious St. Thérèse, whom Almighty God has raised
up to aid and inspire the human family, I implore your
miraculous intercession. You are so powerful in obtaining
every need in body and spirit from the Heart of God. Holy
Mother Church proclaims you "Prodigy of Miracles...the
Greatest Saint of Modern Times."

Now I fervently beseech you to answer my petition (men-
tion your request here) and to carry out your promises of

spending Heaven doing good on earth... of letting fall from Heaven a Shower of Roses.

Little Flower, give me your childlike faith to see the face of God in the people and experiences of my life and to love God with full confidence. St. Thérèse, my Carmelite Sister, I will fulfill your plea "to be made known everywhere," and I will continue to lead others to Jesus through you. Amen.

Prayer of Thanksgiving for the Communion of Saints

Dear Lord Jesus, thank you for the gift of the saints. Help me to remember that the saints are not only holy people up in heaven, but also holy people who can have an important impact on my family's life. Help me to live my life knowing that my time here on earth is a journey to You. Just as the saints found their way to you through prayer, sacrifice and service, help me too to achieve that goal for my children and myself. Please allow the saints to intercede for my family so that we may meet You face to face one day in Heaven. Amen.

So let us keep very small and follow the Little Flower's way of trust, love and joy, and we will fulfill Mother's [Mary's] promise to give saints to Mother Church.
— BLESSED TERESA OF CALCUTTA

A Reflection on the Wisdom of the Saints . . . And being called to be Saints

Blessed Teresa of Calcutta often spoke about the fact that we are all called to be saints. God calls us all to be saints for Him, to bring many souls to Him by our life and our love. When Mother Teresa became a nun, she chose the name Teresa after St. Thérèse, the Little Flower whom she loved. She admired the way St. Thérèse kept a childlike faith and simplicity about her. Mothers, too, are called to a certain kind of simplicity in their lives. By remaining "very small," mothers remain humble and open to God's grace. A mother's "small" acts of love in her family are really huge in God's eyes. Mothers actually help their family to work out their salvation through their dedicated selfless acts of love and guidance in their families.

CHAPTER NINE

Prayerful Days

*Draw near to God and
He will draw near to you.*
— JAS. 4:8

When we pray, the voice of the heart must be heard more than the proceedings from the mouth.
— St. Bonaventure

Personal Prayer

Jesus was known to retreat from the crowds often to pray in solitude, usually on a mountain or in a desert, preferably at night. As mothers, most times we don't have the opportunity to sneak away or retreat to solitude. We know that the care of our family is pretty much all-consuming, and while we cannot go off to the mountain or the desert, we can strive to find the mountain and desert moments in our lives, even in the midst of the busyness. Capture these moments and use them prayerfully. God will reward your efforts. He knows your heart. He knows your desires to come close to Him and bring your family close. He will give you the strength and grace. When your children are older, you will be able to make more opportunities happen for quiet prayer. While the children are small, be content with your busy life, raising your thoughts and heart to God often, thanking Him for His love in your family.

God commands you to pray, but He forbids you to worry.
— St. John Vianney

The Bell Rings

In the quiet of the convent, the bell rings,
Breaking the silence,
Drawing the Sisters to the chapel for prayer.

A mother is called to prayer as the bell rings
    in her home.
It is her baby crying, wanting to nurse,
It is her hungry husband and children, wanting to eat.
All of the various demands and needs of the family
    ring the "bell."

A mother's prayer is most times prayed
Through her loving acts of service to her family.
Rarely does she find a few quiet moments
To lift her heart to Our Lord in peace.
She makes her life a prayer,
And offers her entire day,
With all its turbulence and distractions.

After a long, tiresome day,
When all are in bed,
She will drop down upon weary knees,
Giving thanks to God,
With a promise to serve Him even more
    lovingly tomorrow.

Dear Lord Jesus,
Please continue to hear the prayers of
    mothers
Around the world, pleading for Your help
    for their children.

Prayer is joy, prayer is love, prayer is peace.
                            BLESSED TERESA OF CALCUTTA

Prayer of Spouses for Each Other

Lord Jesus, grant that my spouse and I may have a true understanding love for each other. Please grant us the grace to live with each other in peace and harmony with faith and trust in one another. May we always bear with one another's weaknesses and grow from each other's strengths. Help us to forgive one another's failings and grant us patience, kindness, cheerfulness and the spirit of placing the well being of one another ahead of self.

May our love grow stronger with each passing year. Bring us both closer to You through our love for each other as it grows to perfection. Amen.

Family Prayer

Daily prayer and the reading of the Word of God strengthen the Christian family in charity.
                        — *Catechism of the Catholic Church,*
                            "THE CHRISTIAN FAMILY," 2205

Prayer to the Blessed Mother

Dear Blessed Mother Mary, you know the importance of prayer, and also the importance of being attentive to one's family. Please pray to your Son, Jesus, for me to find the proper balance between the two as I go about my duties in one of the most important vocations ever. Please help me to find opportune moments to pray, raising my heart to God. Help me to desire to quench the "thirst" of Jesus. Please grant me peace in my vocation as mother, so that I may be confident raising my little ones. Please assist me in setting a much-needed example in my family — of praying together and teaching each member to develop a prayer life of their own. Amen.

An approach to prayer with love and patience will work much better with our children than too regimented an approach. You want to teach your family to pray, but you don't want to force it upon them. If you start early when they are young, it will become as natural to them as breathing and will establish a very strong foundation in their lives . . . one they can always lean on. Our Lord tells us He is waiting to hear from us. Anytime, any place.

Refection on
Prayer in the Family

*Consider the gift that prayer really
is . . . God gives us the gift of conversation
with Him. Consider some ways in which to
incorporate more prayer into your life. We can
pray day or night, on our knees or in the car
driving with our children. We can fit in visits to
the Blessed Sacrament where Jesus resides, waiting
for us. We can find prayer time during a walk
out in nature with our children. The blessings
of nature can also help soothe the senses, quiet
the mind, and inspire the soul. Our
prayers need not be formal, but
from the heart.*

CHAPTER TEN

Your Life Is a Prayer

*"And I tell you, Ask, and it will be given you; seek,
and you will find; knock, and it will be opened to you.
For everyone who asks receives, and he who seeks finds;
and to him who knocks, it will be opened."*

— Lk. 11:9-11

Prayer to Jesus Asking for Help to <u>Live</u> My Prayers

Dear Lord Jesus, please help me stay focused in the mothering of my children, knowing the importance of my actions as well as my words in raising them. Help me to see that because I can not easily break away from the task at hand to seek the silence needed to formulate prayers and lift my heart to You, You will help me to transform my life into a prayer. Help me to be patient as my children grow, not trying to rush them, enjoying the time we have together. Please help me to remember that You know how busy I am with my family, and that although I want to devote more time to prayer, I have to be patient with this season of my life, knowing my acts of loving service to my family are very pleasing to You. Please help me to live my prayers, uniting my heart to Yours. Amen.

You must pray the prayer of action, which is the fragrant flower of the soul. A good man [woman] is a prayer.
— ST. CATHERINE OF SIENA

The fruit of silence is prayer.
The fruit of prayer is faith.
The fruit of faith is love.
The fruit of love is service.
The fruit of service is peace.
— BLESSED TERESA OF CALCUTTA

"Therefore, I tell you, whatever you ask in prayer, believe that you receive it, and you will."
— MK. 11:24

The Rosary, One Decade at a Time

Because caring for my family
Demands my full attention,
Please, Lord, accept my Rosary
One decade at a time.

When the children are fed and dishes washed
And baby is asleep,
I can borrow some time now to kneel down
And pray a decade of the Rosary.

And later, as I sit and rock and nurse my baby,
My heart goes out to You, my Lord,
As I recite the second decade.

When my baby cries and I attempt to calm her
By walking with her,
My fingers will be a substitute
For the next ten beads of the next decade.

After dinner, I can gather together my flock
To kneel together for family prayer.
We will recite a decade along with our evening prayers.

Finally, when the day is finished,
And all are in bed,
With a quiet sigh,
I settle down to complete my Rosary to You.

Prayer to Jesus in Thanksgiving

Dear Jesus, thank You for the many blessings of every day, blessings I sometimes don't recognize. Help me to find opportune moments to gaze upon You. Help me and my children come closer to You.

A Reflection on Living the Prayer

Take some time to reflect on what it means to live a prayer. When obstacles get in the path of prayer, I should not give in to discouragement or give up my efforts. What does it mean to live a life of a holy example to your family? Consider what can be done to capture opportunities to pray throughout every day. What can be done to transform your life into a prayer pleasing to Our Lord? Ask God to help empty your heart of all the clutter that gets in the way of coming closer to Him.

CHAPTER ELEVEN

Forever a Mother

She looks well to the ways of her household,
and does not eat the bread of idleness.
— PROV. 31:27

A mother is always a mother, no matter how old her children are. When they are young, she is ever attentive to their care and their well being. As they grow, her care for them continues as they learn to navigate life a little on their own. But, even when her children are adults, a mother's love and concern and even her guidance will be ever ready, always available. Her love never stops, only increases.

Dear Lord Jesus, thank You for the love You have put in my heart for my children. Please help me to have a never-ending influence on my children, even as they are older and on their own. Remind me, please, that my prayers for them are an integral part of the means to their salvation.

Dear Blessed Mother Mary, create in me a vessel of joy to be given to all around me.

Always a Mother

Once a mother, always a mother.
A mother to her beloved children
And a motherly influence to many more,
A shining example to others,
Her love is a shelter.
Dedicated love,
Serving,
Loving.

Dear Blessed Mother Mary, help me
to see how my role in life as a mother
extends to many others, not only my children.
Please grant me the graces I most need
to be a shining example to bring many
souls to your Son, Jesus.

The Blessings of Every Day

Thank you, dear Lord for my life,
And the blessings of every day.
Thank you for the children You have blessed me with.
Help me to remember that they are on loan to me,
So that I may help mold their consciences
And allow them to grow.
Teach me to teach them
As I strive to help them find
The true essence of themselves.
Help me to find the opportunities
To grow along with them
As we journey through life
In the profound blessing of the family.

Jesus is pleased to come to us
As the truth to be told
And the life to be lived,
As the light to be lighted
And the love to be loved,

As the joy to be given
And the peace to be spread.
— **Blessed Teresa of Calcutta**

Prayer to the Blessed Mother

Dear Blessed Mother Mary, help me to be content in my vocation as mother. Help me to see that my role in helping light my children's "lamps" is really an awesome task of immeasurable value. It is a role I shall live out my entire life for my children, and even in eternity. Please grant me your grace and continue to protect my family always from the snares of the devil. Amen.

A Reflection on Your Forever Role

Reflect on your forever role as a mother. Before your children's hearts began to beat within your womb, you were a mother. From the moment of conception, God blessed you with new life and the abounding graces of a mother. He continues to bless you today.

CHAPTER TWELVE

Seasons in a
Mother's Life

*For everything there is a season, and a time
for every matter under heaven.*
— ECCLES. 3:1

Every Season Is a Blessing

Throughout a mother's life are seasons interwoven in the tapestry of motherhood: seasons of joy, sorrow, and thanksgiving; seasons of busyness and exhaustion, of quiet and calmness. When children are very young, life is extremely full of their unending care and chores, along with the continuous joy that accompanies them. As they grow, life becomes even busier, if that could be possible. When, with bittersweet emotion, they embark on their own journeys, the mother's pace lets up a little, affording more time for quiet prayer and ministry to others. Every season is a blessing as a mother grows in holiness with her children.

Dear Lord Jesus, thank You for my life as a mother. Thank You for all of the blessings and love You have bestowed upon me. My heart swells with joy, happiness, and peace contemplating the great love that compelled You to bless me with the gifts of my children. Thank You for the gift of faith You have given me. Please increase it in my heart as I pray for my children.

God comes to us in the things we know best and can verify most easily, the things of our everyday life.
— POPE JOHN PAUL II

Prayer For Mothers

God, our Father,
Full of compassion for all who turn to you
In their hour of need,
You gave St. Monica
The wonderful grace of sanctity
As wife and mother.
Through prayer and perseverance,
She won for you, Lord,
Both her husband and her wayward son, Augustine.
Grant to all mothers
The same patience and prayer-filled concern,
So that your Son's love
May become manifest in the family. Amen.

A Family Prayer

Lord, bless our family: all of us now together, those far away, all who are gone back to you. May we know joy. May we bear our sorrows in patience. Let love guide our understanding of each other. Let us be grateful to each other. We have all made each other what we are. O Family of Jesus, watch over our family. Amen.

Thank you, Lord, for coming
to me always in the things
of my everyday life.

Not Perfection, Just Peace

I have come to realize that
My house may never be perfectly clean,
Or aesthetically correct.
I may not always be up to date
With the latest fashion.
Perhaps my nails are not always nicely manicured.
But I do have consolation in knowing
My children are happy
And on the correct path,
Because I put in the time,
The patience, the sacrifice, and the love.
Thank you, Lord for the grace
To see the meaning and significance in a mother's love.

Thank you, Blessed Mother Mary, my mother in Heaven, for accompanying me always on my journey throughout motherhood. Remind me to call upon you for peace and protection for my family. Please keep us all under your motherly protection.

Prayer to Jesus

Thank you, dear Lord, for the miraculous vocation of motherhood You have blessed me with. At times, I may not be able to fathom the intensity of the miracles that are worked in human hearts throughout the seasons of my vocation as mother. By Your grace and love for me, I trust that I act as Your instrument in this world – first to my own family, and then, reaching out to others. Please continue to work through me as I work out my own salvation and that of my family. Help me to lead others to You by my life and love.

A Reflection on a Mother's Life

*Reflect on how our Lord has truly blessed
you throughout your motherhood journey.
Consider how you can strive to find beauty and
wisdom in your vocation and in life. Take time to
truly thank God for all of His gifts, especially for
putting you right there in the midst of your family.
He has specifically chosen you to mother your children.*

*Even though we know a mother's job is very much one of
service, don't forget there is a tremendous amount of
room for joy within your vocation as well. Try to leave the
past to yesterday, and don't waste time worrying about
tomorrow. Live now, in the present moment, cherishing
the time as you mother your children. Do your best
not to allow the weight of responsibility or fatigue
to overcome your joy; laughter and fun are gifts
from God, as well, and help us maintain
our balance. So remember
to laugh!*

"Be Not Afraid."

Throughout his Papacy, Pope John Paul II spoke these simple, yet powerful, words often. He spoke them for the first time publicly on the steps of St. Peter's, when he became the Pope. Mothers can take these words to heart throughout their vocation, knowing that there is nothing to fear. God is truly with us. We are right where we should be — in the midst of our families, in the heart of our homes, lovingly praying for our children's salvation.

A mother should "be not afraid" to be that inspiring example to her family, and to others, throughout her motherly journey. Ask Jesus to show you how to find the "quiet" moments during the busyness of your life in which to retreat to your heart to contemplate Him and His love. There, Jesus can speak to you, transforming your soul, as you become united to Him, all the while, drawing your children to Him, as well.

Enjoy and savor your vocation of love, the marvelous pilgrimage of motherhood.

Jesus, I trust in You.